Contents

INTRODUCTION

LEARN ABOUT amazing spaceplanes ...

In the future, space travel may be as common as aeroplane flights are today. Getting there will be a big challenge. Even a simple space mission costs millions of pounds. Distances are so vast that visiting the closest planets takes months.

New technology will be needed to overcome all these problems. Yet just 50 years ago, humans had hardly started to explore space. Technology can change quickly. Read on to find out what might be ahead in our quest to reach the stars.

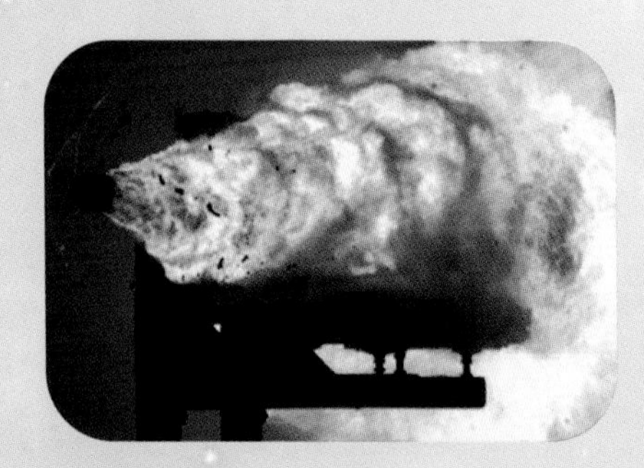

... deadly weapons ...

... crazy facts about planets ...

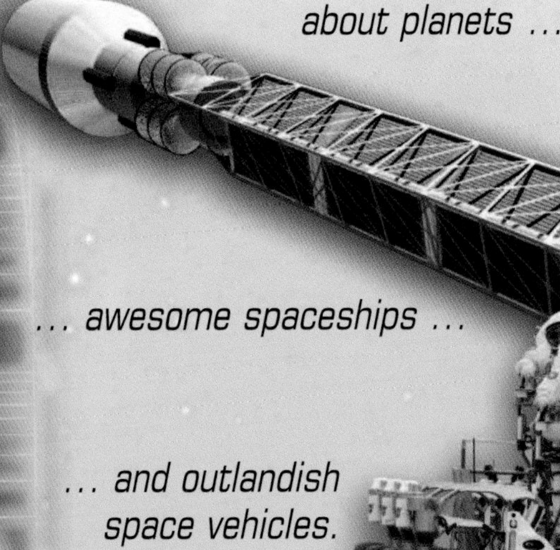

... awesome spaceships ...

... and outlandish space vehicles.

"Welcome to Spaceport B. Would passengers for the Moon Shuttle please go to Dock 4. The arrival of Mars SuperCruiser 776 has been delayed by 39 hours due to a **cosmic ray** storm. **Freighter** M41 from the platinum mine on asteroid Psyche is boarding. Travellers for the Saturn Rings Tour must check their space suits before departure. Have a great trip!"

The story so far

Storytellers have dreamed of space travel for centuries. In the 1950s, new technology and a better understanding of space helped scientists to turn fiction into reality.

Governments usually paid for early research into space travel. They wanted to be the first to put objects and people in space. Today, private companies also develop and sell new space travel technology.

Rocket launch

Rocket technology makes space travel possible. Rockets have been around since the first fireworks were invented, but a special kind of rocket was needed for space travel. Rockets that burn liquid fuel were developed in the early twentieth century, and used to launch the first satellite into orbit in 1957.

People in space

The next challenge was putting a person in space. In 1961, Yuri Gagarin became the first man in space. Since then, many astronauts have "walked" in space and even visited the Moon in 1969, 1971 and 1972.

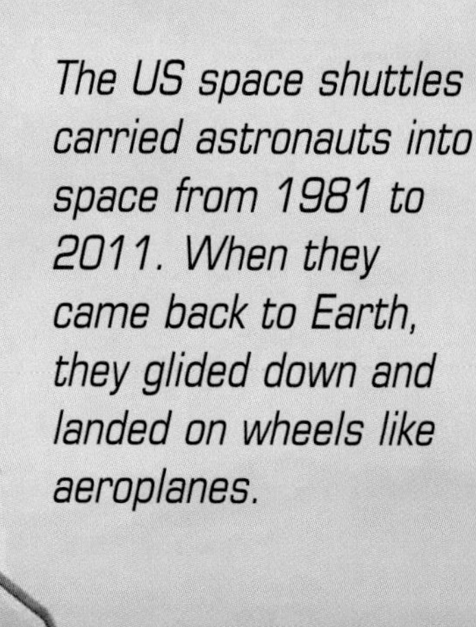

The US space shuttles carried astronauts into space from 1981 to 2011. When they came back to Earth, they glided down and landed on wheels like aeroplanes.

Different astronauts lived and worked on board the Russian Mir space station for 15 years. In 2001 it was taken out of orbit, and it burned up as a fireball as it fell to Earth.

Bases in space

The first space stations were launched in the early 1970s. They orbit Earth, providing a base for astronauts to carry out research into space. Other satellites, such as the Hubble Space Telescope, are not manned. Hubble gathers information about space and beams it back to Earth.

Visiting the solar system

Space probes have been sent across our **solar system**, to find out more about Earth's nearest planets and star. Some have landed on the surface of other worlds, beaming back amazing pictures. Despite these amazing journeys, space travel has only just begun!

The rovers Spirit and Opportunity landed on Mars in 2004. The rover Curiosity was launched in 2011.

FUTURE LAUNCH

The "space rockets" that you see on the news are actually launch vehicles. Their job is to carry smaller craft into space. In years to come, they may not have rocket engines at all.

*This Boeing Delta IV launcher uses extra boosters to lift heavy **cargoes**.*

booster rockets

HEAVY LIFTERS

Launch vehicles (LVs) burn huge amounts of fuel to reach speeds of 11.2 kilometres per second, the speed needed to escape Earth's **gravity**. Once they have carried their cargo into space, the rocket engines become space junk. This makes them expensive to use. Small LVs can carry one or two satellites into space. Heavy-lift LVs can carry more than 90 metric tons into orbit.

Several companies are developing reusable rocket boosters. Instead of being abandoned in space, they would fly back to Earth to be used again.

MASS DRIVERS

One alternative to a rocket engine may be the "mass driver". It works like a superspeed **maglev train**, using powerful electrical magnets to catapult a launch vehicle into space.

A Moon-based mass driver would hurl launch vehicles along a long track and up into space.

"Changing the way rockets are designed would pave the way to transporting more people into space. It could lead to a next generation type of space shuttle carrying up to 100 people." ***Buzz Aldrin, the second man to walk on the Moon***

Airports of the future may have spaceport terminals too.

"Seemed like a good idea ..."

Science fiction author Jules Verne described a "Moon gun" in his story "From the Earth to the Moon" (1865). It shot a spacecraft like a ball from a giant cannon. In reality, the sudden force from speeding up so fast would kill any passengers!

Space base

A space station is a permanent base in space, where astronauts can live and carry out research over many months or years. The first successful base for humans in space was Russia's Salyut 3 in 1974. Today the International Space Station (ISS) is 20 times bigger with room for six crew.

The Jules Verne ATV (Automated Transfer Vehicle) is a robot "space tug" that carries supplies up to the ISS.

Modular design

The ISS is made up of many different sections or modules. Each one is carried up by launch vehicles and then fixed together in orbit. Electricity comes from 16 huge **solar panels** with an area bigger than nine tennis courts.

Engineers began to build the ISS in orbit in 1998. It has more than 20 main parts, or modules.

Space elevator

Space bases of the future might be jumping-off places for visits to faraway planets. A space elevator would act like an enormous airport walkway, carrying passengers 36,000 kilometres from Earth's surface up to a space port. Just don't look down!

A space elevator is an enormously long cable stretching from Earth's surface to an orbiting base. A lift rides up and down the cable.

Space motel

Space tourists can stay on the ISS, but a ticket costs millions of pounds. Other companies are designing "space motels" that could make it cheaper to have a holiday in space. Bigelow's space station will be built from modules that are blown up to full size in space.

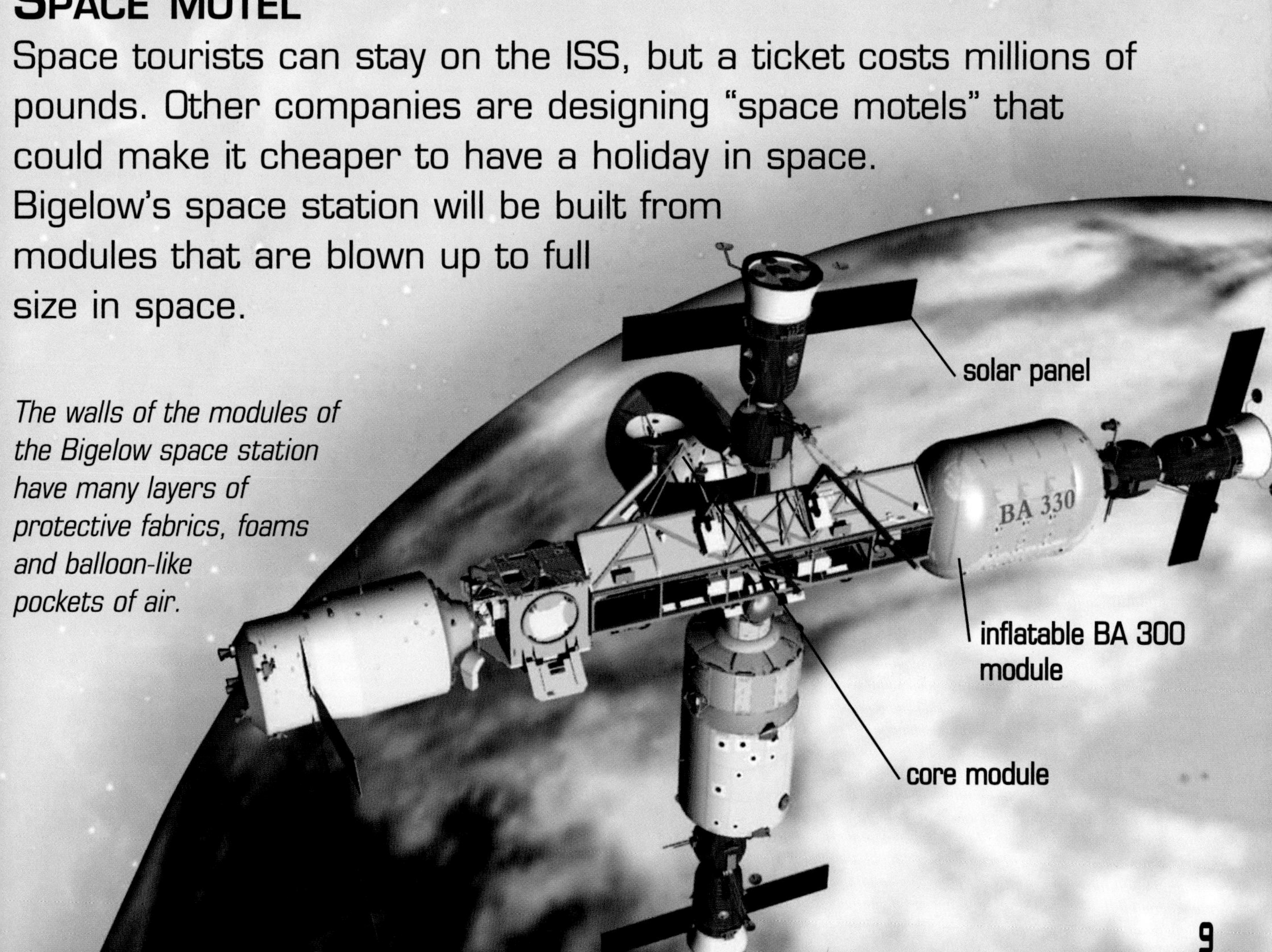

The walls of the modules of the Bigelow space station have many layers of protective fabrics, foams and balloon-like pockets of air.

SPACEPLANES

Launch vehicles are used to carry things into space. In the future, a small amount of cargo could be carried in spaceplanes. These will take off and land like aeroplanes, but fly much higher.

Skylon would be able to carry 11 metric tons of cargo, or up to 24 passengers, into orbit. Then it would fly back to a runway and refuel for the next mission. It could do this up to 200 times.

RETURN TICKET

Most launch vehicles are abandoned after they have carried their cargo into space. There is no way of getting them back to Earth, so they drift away as space junk. Spaceplanes would reduce waste by making many trips into space and back.

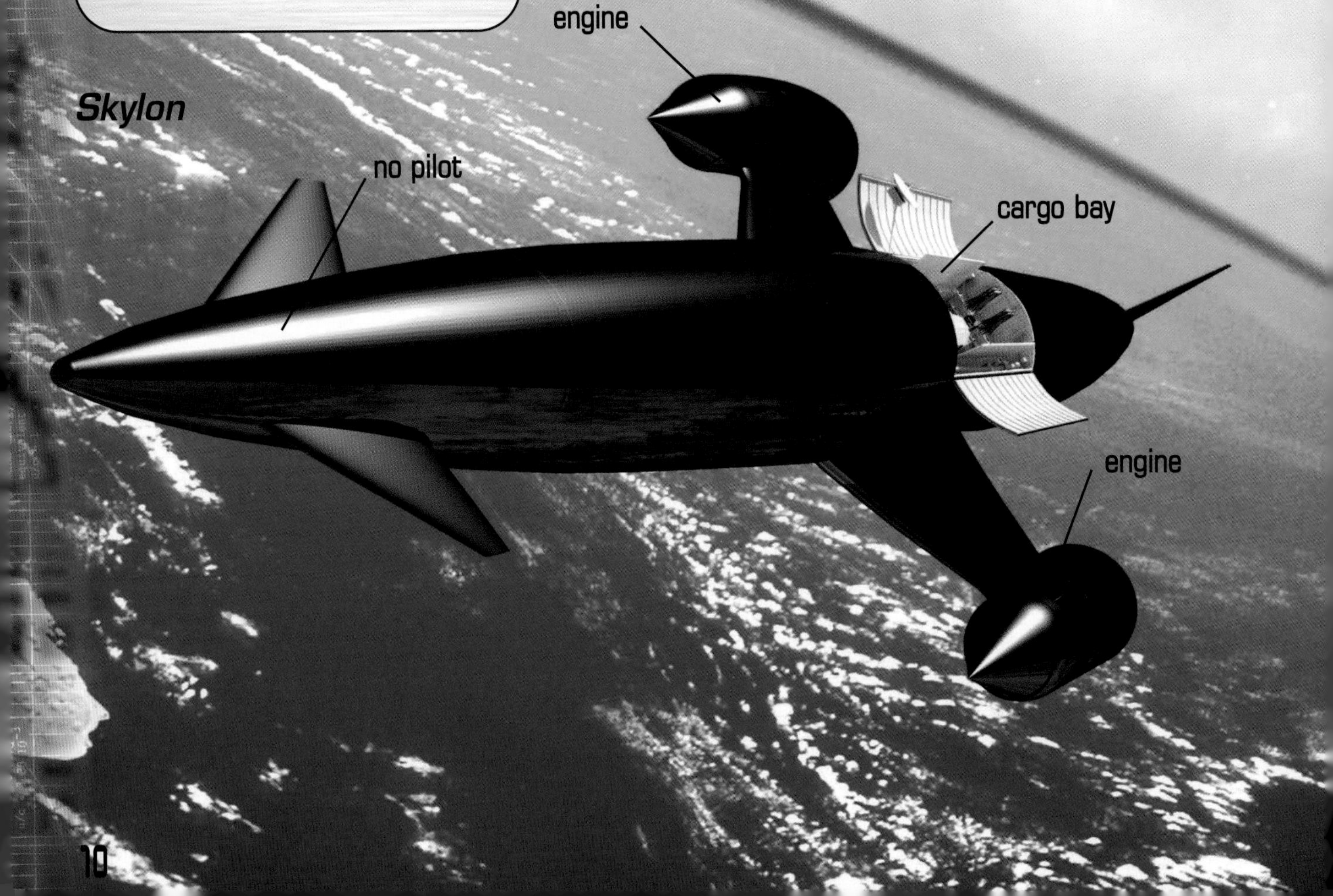

Skylon

Part engine, part rocket

Spaceplanes will have **jet engines**, like aeroplanes. These engines need **oxygen** to burn their fuel. While they are close to Earth, spaceplanes like Skylon will use oxygen from the air to burn fuel. They will use rocket engines in space, where there is no air.

EADS Astrium have designed a spaceplane to take tourists 100 kilometres above Earth's surface. It will have jet engines and rocket engines.

"Seemed like a good idea ..."

In the 1970s, VentureStar was supposed to bring the Space Age to ordinary travellers with joyrides into orbit. After more than £770 million, several test failures of scaled-down models, and lack of interest, it was cancelled.

How scramjets work

Scramjets are very high-speed jet engines that use oxygen from the air to burn fuel. Unlike a normal jet engine they have no moving parts. This is good for future space travel, as there are no mechanics in orbit. One problem is that scramjets don't start working until they are moving very fast.

In 2004, NASA's X-43 scramjet test plane reached more than 12,000 kilometres per hour. But it had to be boosted by a rocket before the scramjet started working.

Star wars

Science fiction films love to imagine human heroes battling alien invaders in space. But spacecraft are already being used to combat enemies here on Earth.

Railgun tests in the US have fired test "bullets" at more than 9,656 kilometres per hour.

Spies in space

Space satellites have the best view of our planet. They can carry powerful cameras, heat sensors, movement detectors and other equipment to spot tanks, missiles, enemy aeroplanes and warships. They also detect radio signals from possible enemies. Almost nothing can be hidden from these silent spies in space.

The railgun

A railgun would use electrical and magnetic forces to speed a "bullet" between railway-type metal tracks. The tracks would aim the bullet at targets in space, such as spy satellites or space weapons.

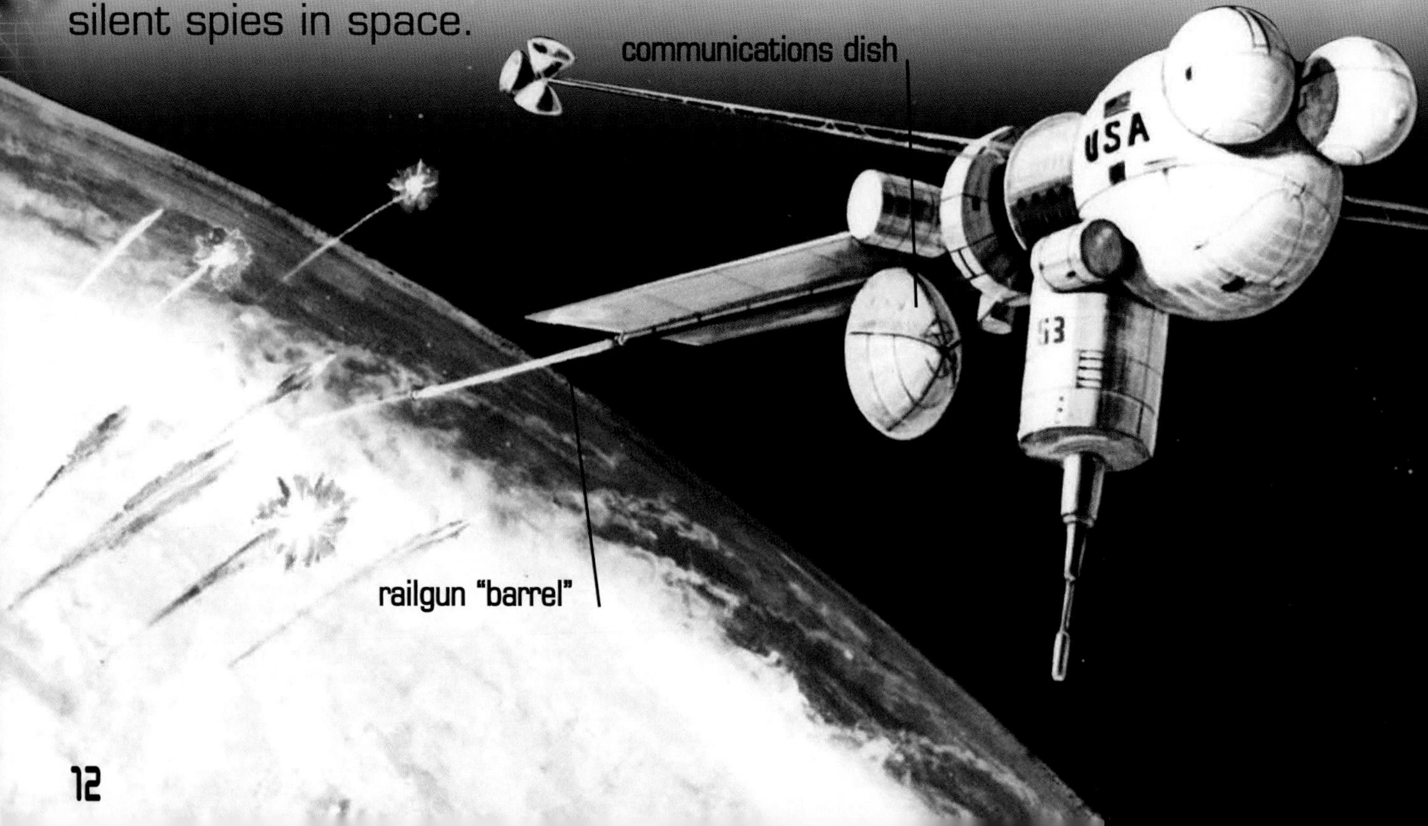

Boiled into bits

The best space weapon would be super-powered **lasers**. They would fire beams of light with enough energy to heat the target so quickly that it boils, and blasts itself apart. Successful tests of laser weapons have been carried out on Earth.

"Seemed like a good idea ..."

The US Air Force began designing a military spaceplane in 1957. The X-20 Dyna-Soar was designed for missions such as spying and bombing enemy satellites. But the plan was abandoned in 1963, just as building work on the spacecraft began.

Scientists have worked out that one space laser could destroy up to 20 enemy satellites or weapons.

MOON TOWN

With today's rockets and spacecraft, the Moon is almost 3 days away. Faster transport technology could shorten the trip to a few hours, and make the Moon a great jumping-off place to reach other planets.

A NASA concept for the beginnings of a Moon base.

FUTURE FRONTIER

The Moon would make a good base for space travel because its gravity is weaker than Earth's. This means its pull on other objects is weaker. Launch vehicles blasting off the Moon could be much smaller and more **efficient**. The Moon also has useful minerals that could be mined to build shelters and spacecraft. Recent discoveries show that there is even some water on the Moon, which would be essential to support human life.

Solar panels could make plenty of electricity on the Moon where there are no clouds to block the Sun's rays.

Astronauts will need tough vehicles to get around on the Moon. Future Moon buggies will have solar panels to recharge their batteries for long trips.

Each set of wheels has separate suspension**, to travel over bumpy surfaces.**

LIVING CONDITIONS

Future Moon bases will need air-filled spaces for people to live in. The temperature inside will have to be carefully controlled as it ranges from -166°C to 115°C outside. The Eden Project in Cornwall shows how climate can be controlled inside huge glass and metal domes.

The climate inside the Eden Project domes is hot and wet enough for a rainforest to grow.

Life on Mars

More spacecraft have been sent to Mars, our nearest planet, than any other planet. No signs of life have been spotted yet. But there could be life on Mars in 50 years, if humans begin to live on the "Red Planet".

In 2008 the US Phoenix lander found water on Mars, frozen into ice at the poles.

Seeing red

With today's technology the trip to Mars takes more than 3 months. So far, no human has been sent on this long journey. New kinds of space transport may include nuclear-powered engines that could speed a crew to Mars and back by 2035.

*Astronauts would need an air supply on Mars. The planet's thin **atmosphere** is mostly deadly carbon dioxide gas.*

Terraforming

It would not be possible to take along all the air, water, food and other supplies that astronauts would need on Mars. Instead, humans could change the conditions in their base area to be like those on Earth. This is known as "terraforming". Soil, ice, rocks and minerals found on Mars would be used to make water, air and building materials. Indoor farms would be set up to grow food.

"Seemed like a good idea ..."

In 1877 astronomer Giovanni Schiaparelli saw "channels" on Mars through his telescope. The idea grew that Martians had built canals to farm crops – but it was a trick of the light.

Burning minerals found on Mars could create greenhouse gases to trap the Sun's heat, making the planet warm enough for humans.

Mars outpost

The first bases on Mars would be sent ready-built in a giant cargo spaceliner built in Earth's orbit. People would follow once the base was safely in place.

ESA's plan for a Mars base has areas to live and work in, with satellite dishes for talking to Earth.

laboratory

satellite dish

habitation pod

esa

OFF-WORLD MINING

Asteroids like Eros tumble slowly as they orbit, making it tricky to land on them.

Holidays in space would be fun, but future space transport could help to solve serious problems too. Asteroids, planets and comets are rich in precious resources that are running out on Earth.

SPACE TREASURE

Space probes and telescope studies show that some asteroids are rich in metals such as gold, platinum and nickel. These are rare and expensive on Earth. Therefore one day it may be worth sending mining spaceships, crews and space freighters.

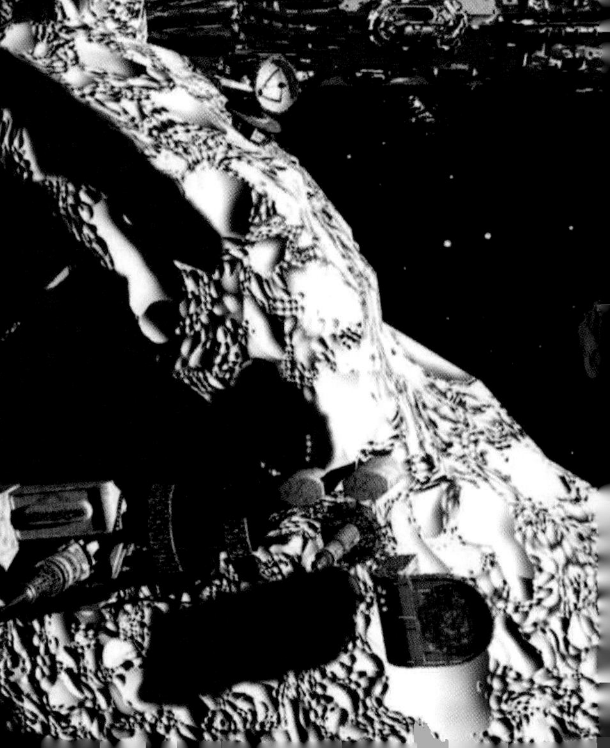

Space miners would need huge robot diggers, manned control craft and giant processing ships to extract valuable minerals from the rocks.

Moon mining

In the future, much of Earth's energy could be produced by nuclear fusion reactors. These would use a material called helium-3 as fuel. Helium-3 is very rare on Earth, but there is plenty on the Moon.

Helium-3 might be mined on the Moon by 2050.

Space freighters

Robotic freighters could ship hundreds of tons of precious materials back to Earth. With no crew to keep alive, they would not need to carry oxygen or supplies. All the space on board could be used to carry cargo.

Japan's H-2 TV robot craft supplies the ISS. It could be the basis for future designs 500 times bigger.

Space probes

Space probes are unmanned spacecraft operated by remote control from Earth. The latest probes also have powerful computers on board, which can make decisions by themselves.

The BepiColombo probe will begin travelling to Mercury, the closest planet to the Sun, in 2015. When it arrives in 2020, it will split into different parts, each with a different job to do.

1. This orbiter will study Mercury's magnetic field.
2. This orbiter will study the scorching planet itself.
3. These are the state-of-the-art ion engines.

New Horizons

The NASA space probe New Horizons will be the first spacecraft to explore the dwarf planet Pluto, when it arrives in 2015. Pluto is so far from Earth that radio signals from the probe will take 5 hours to travel back to operators on Earth. New Horizons' computer "brain" will need to control the spacecraft in an emergency.

NASA scientists work on New Horizons in a clean room to avoid getting Earth germs on to the spacecraft. The probe's journey to Pluto will take 9 years.

Sun probe

NASA's Solar Probe Plus is designed to get closer to the Sun than any other spacecraft. It will set off for the Sun's atmosphere by 2018. A heavy shield will protect the probe from heat that would fry humans.

The equipment of Solar Probe Plus is positioned to stay in the shield's shadow.

"Seemed like a good idea ..."

It is easier for an on-board computer to send data back to Earth than it is to bring back samples from space. In 2004 the Genesis probe flew past Earth to drop off a capsule of material from deep space. The parachute failed, and the container crash-landed at 322 kilometres per hour.

LANDERS AND ROVERS

Space probes collect information about other worlds by flying close to them, or spending time in orbit. Landers go one better by touching down on the surface. Best of all are rovers, which travel around on wheels or legs.

The six-legged Athlete rover is being developed for Moon-walking. It will simply step over boulders.

TOUCHDOWN!

The first challenge for a lander or rover is touching down without crashing. Parachutes only work if there is an atmosphere. For planets, moons and asteroids without thick atmospheres, cushion-like airbags could help landers to "bounce-down".

At almost 1 metric ton, the Mars Science Laboratory is the largest ever rover planned for visiting Mars. One day it may help space scientists to find out if there has ever been life on Mars.

cameras

instruments to monitor the weather

radio antenna

long-lasting power source

robot arm

The Rosetta probe should meet Comet Churyumov-Gerasimenko in 2014. It will release its dustbin-sized lander to land gently in the comet's tiny gravity.

Power sources

Some landers and rovers have solar panels, with rechargeable batteries for when it's dark. But these run out quickly on planets with nights that last for many Earth months or years. A special generator can make electricity using **radioactive** fuel, even in the dark.

"Seemed like a good idea ..."

Beagle 2 tried to land on Mars in 2003. Its three-part landing system of heat shield, parachutes and airbags worked well in tests. But as it approached Mars, contact was lost. No information was ever sent back to Earth, so the mission failed.

The Scarab Moon lander is being tested on Earth. It drills holes and crushes the rock samples to test them for minerals.

Space tourism

Time for a future holiday? Don't forget to pack your clothes, camera, sunscreen, hard hat, pressure suit and deep space survival kit! Space tourism will be a reality 50 years from now, but only for the very rich.

Thrill seekers

Back in 2001, US engineer Denis Tito became the first paying space tourist. For £12 million, he spent seven days in the ISS, circling Earth 128 times. Since then, more than seven people have made the trip. A more affordable option is a short hop to the edge of Earth's atmosphere, in a spaceship like Virgin Galactic's SpaceShipTwo.

SpaceShipTwo will be launched from a "mothership" which takes off like a normal aeroplane. The smaller craft will then break free, and carry six passengers up to the edge of space.

STAYING SAFE IN SPACE

Moon visits may begin in the second half of this century, but tourists hoping to see the red glow of Mars, or the swirling storms of Jupiter, will have to wait until the 2100s. Their bodies would have to get used to the feeling of weightlessness in space. They may have to make long trips in a very deep sleep. There are no hospitals in space. Travellers will need careful medical check-ups before they go.

The Dragon Capsule is another spacecraft that could take paying passengers on short sightseeing trips into orbit. Its main job will be carrying crew and supplies to the ISS.

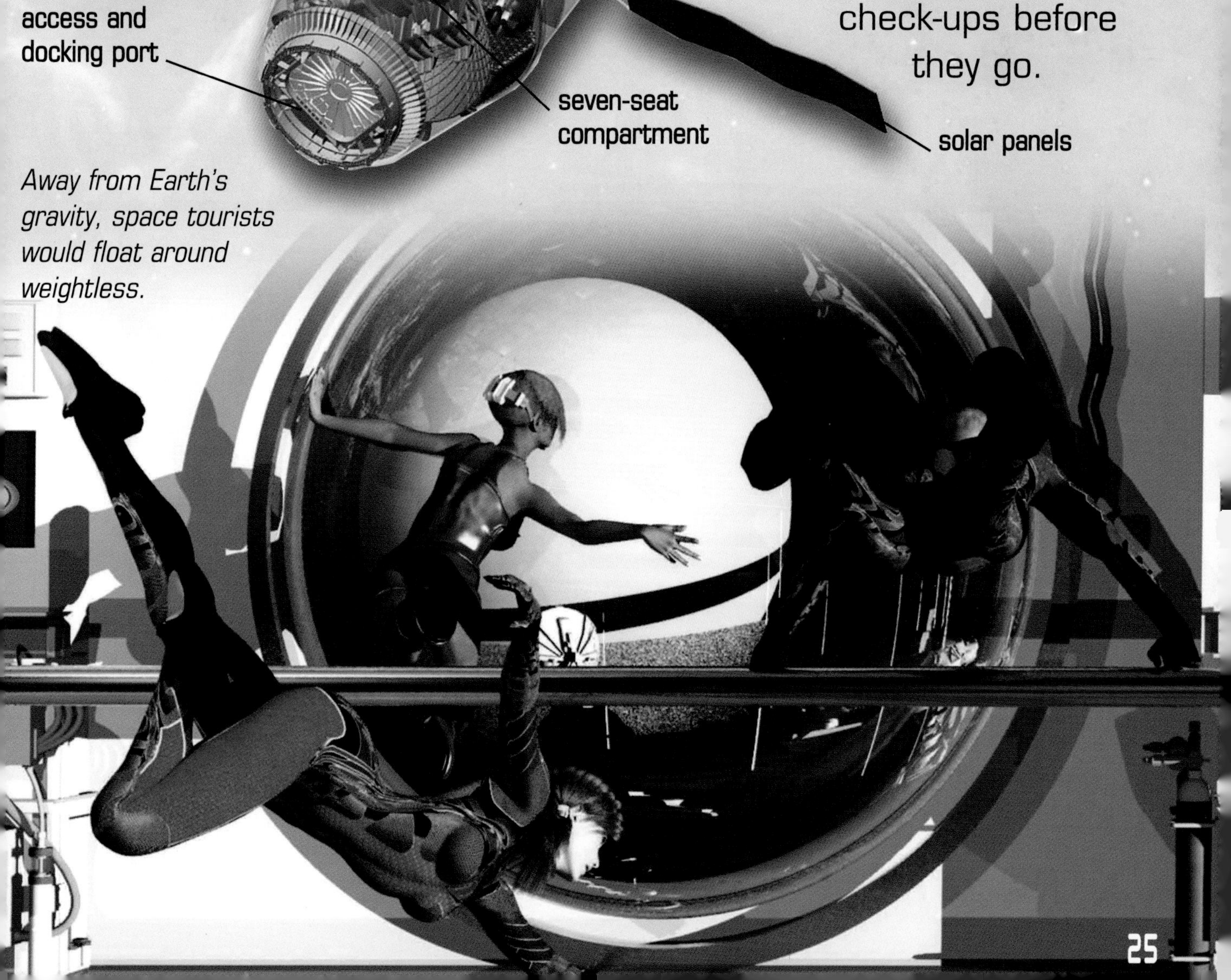

Away from Earth's gravity, space tourists would float around weightless.

Aliens ahoy!

No signs of alien life have been found in our solar system, but there are likely to be other forms of life somewhere in the universe. A few may be far more advanced than us. They could be on their way here, right now!

Keep it clean

When spacecraft bring samples back to Earth, they must go through careful checks in "clean rooms" in case they carry unknown forms of life. Human spacecraft are made perfectly clean before they launch, so that they don't carry Earth's **microbes** to other worlds.

*A **meteorite** from Mars was found in Antarctica in 1984. It was probably knocked off a planet by a bigger meteorite impact. Tiny shapes in it could be fossils of simple Martian life-forms.*

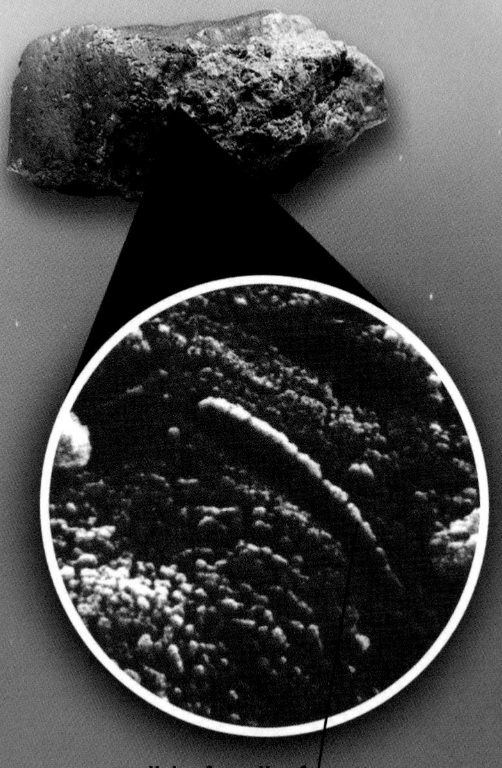

possible fossil of Mars microbe

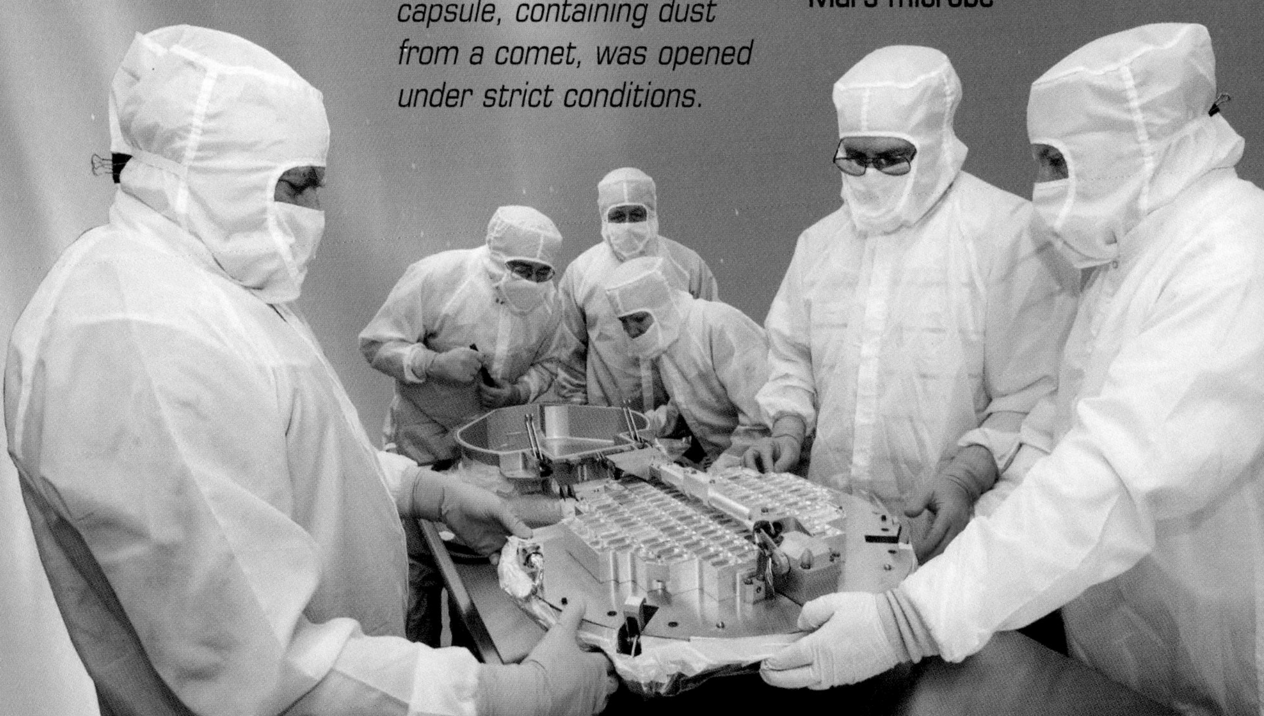

In 2006 the Stardust space probe's return capsule, containing dust from a comet, was opened under strict conditions.

Science-fiction films and books often imagine powerful aliens blasting Earth from giant spaceships. However, aliens may well turn out to be friendly explorers, searching for signs of life.

Travel to the stars

The near future may bring trips to nearby planets and their moons. To visit the nearest stars would take technology that we can only dream of.

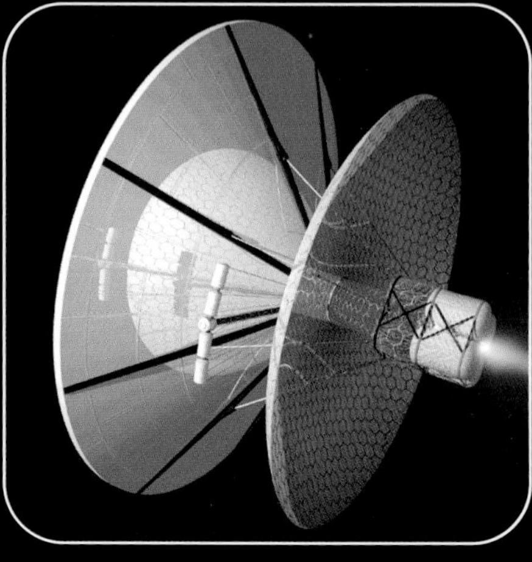

This spacecraft would scoop up space dust using a huge magnet, and push it out of the back to drive the craft forwards.

An antimatter engine such as on this rocket could produce a huge amount of thrust, but antimatter fuel is difficult to make.

"Seemed like a good idea ..."

Project Orion was a 1960's idea for a rocket powered by tiny nuclear explosions. These mini "bombs" would be set off every second behind the spacecraft, pushing it along. However, it would have produced dangerous nuclear waste.

Star drives

After the Sun, our nearest star is Proxima Centauri. The fastest possible journey we can predict with tomorrow's science is about 100 years. Even at the speed of light (300,000 kilometres per second) it would take over 4 years. To make star travel possible, future scientists will need to invent some breathtaking new technologies.

Future spacecraft may face dangers that no one knows about yet.

Wormholes

Space scientists are still learning about the amazing objects and events of deep space. They think that there may be places called "wormholes", where huge amounts of energy and gravity "fold" space into a funnel. If these do exist, a future spaceship may be able to enter at one end and pop out of the other in a split second – far across the galaxy.

GLOSSARY

ATMOSPHERE
gases surrounding the Earth or other planets

CARGOES
goods carried by ships, planes or other vehicles

COSMIC RAY
stream of high-energy particles that enter Earth's atmosphere from outer space

EFFICIENT
working in a way that gets results, with little wasted effort

FREIGHTER
vehicle for taking goods from one place to another

GRAVITY
force by which all objects are attracted to each other

JET ENGINES
engines that cause forward movement by the power of a stream of gases being forced out in the opposite direction

LASERS
devices that give out intense beams of light

MAGLEV TRAIN
type of high-speed train that runs on magnets

METEORITE
space rock

MICROBES
life forms that can only be seen under a microscope

OXYGEN
gas that makes up about 20 per cent of Earth's atmosphere. Most living things need oxygen

RADIOACTIVE
gives out waves of energy

ROCKET ENGINES
jet engines that are driven by reaction

SOLAR PANELS
panels of cells that convert light from the Sun into energy

SOLAR SYSTEM
the Sun together with the planets, asteroids and comets that orbit around it

SPACE PROBES
unmanned exploratory spaceships

SUSPENSION
parts of a vehicle that maintain flexibility between the wheels and the frame

Index